For Jim Mann,

Your very own
copy — i chop i
too much thinking —
too i frightful &
blessed for yourself.

Thoughtful Mr. Mann
blessed for passionage —
don't be a stranger.

love & prayers,

Ruth

Alison   Jackie   Kim
                    Brendan